How to Kill Your Girlfriend's Cat

How to Kill Your Girlfriend's Cat

DR. ROBERT DAPHNE

WITH ILLUSTRATIONS BY SUSAN DAVIS

A DOLPHIN BOOK

DOUBLEDAY

NEW YORK ▲ LONDON ▲ TORONTO

SYDNEY ▲ AUCKLAND

DESIGNED BY
DIANE STEVENSON / SNAP•HAUS GRAPHICS

A Dolphin Book
Published by Doubleday, a division of
Bantam Doubleday Dell Publishing Group, Inc.,
666 Fifth Avenue, New York, New York 10103
Dolphin, Doubleday and the portrayal of two dolphins
are trademarks of Doubleday, a division of
Bantam Doubleday Dell Publishing Group, Inc.

Library of Congress Cataloging-in-Publication Data

Daphne, Robert.
How to kill your girlfriend's cat.

"A Dolphin book."
1. Cats—Humor.   I. Title.
PN6162.D346   1988   818'.5402   88-7115
ISBN 0-385-24648-X

ALL RIGHTS RESERVED
PRINTED IN THE UNITED STATES OF AMERICA
September 1988
First Edition

BG

For Louis. Not the book, the techniques
— Dr. Robert Daphne

For my mother, who *really* hated cats,

and for Bob, whose personal feeling for cats is
evident in a number of the following ways
— Susan Davis

INTRODUCTION

A fter all these years, you've met the girl of your dreams. She's beautiful. Brilliant. Fun. Sexy. No old boyfriends darken the picture. No mother shows up six times a day. No annoying habits intrude. Unlike your last girlfriend, she does not practice the Ninja Death Strike while asleep.

The fact is, you've fallen in love. Now only one problem threatens your bliss. You ignored it at first, but that phase is over. You can't stand it anymore. Your girlfriend has a cat.

Because of this pet your couch (it used to be a couch) looks like shredded wheat. You can't sleep at night (the cat is on your face). There's white hair in the bed, kitchen, clothing drawers, medicine cabinet, locked suitcases, washing machine, hard-to-clean areas behind the bookcase, and even in your shirts when you put them on.

People constantly ask you if you "cut yourself shaving." You sneezed in your boss's face the day before salary raises were to be announced. Your girlfriend has taken to lying. "There's no smell in the kitchen," she says. The only baseball trophy you ever won "fell" off the bookcase and shattered. Your girlfriend won't go away even for a weekend because "Louis gets lonely." And if you have a fight, she scoops up the cat, ignores you, and walks around the apartment crooning, "Oh my boyyy, my onnnne. I love you. [kiss] Do you love me? [kiss] I kiss you, Louis, Louis, Louis."

More. Your expensive Persian rug, given to you by a Kurdish chief, looks like it was used in a Ginsu knives demonstration. When your girlfriend leaves the apartment for just ten minutes, Louis cries piteously, rubs gently and winningly against your ankles, and slashes the top of your thumb off when you reach to pet him.

Your girlfriend insists all her *old* boyfriends loved Louis, played with him, crumpled up little paper balls and Louis fetched them, instead of lying there the way he does when you try it. But one day you run into the old boyfriends in a record store and they say, "Does she still have Louis? She does? Hahahaha!"

You. Hate. The. Cat. You tell yourself if you really loved your girlfriend you would learn to love Louis too, but an idea comes into your head. In horror you brush it away. You've always thought of yourself as a good citizen, a be-kind-to-animals type of guy. But the idea won't leave you alone. You daydream about putting Drano in the liver snacks. You start to have sympathy for murderers in movies. You notice other guys, hundreds of guys on the street with the same distracted look. Finally you decide to do it. Commit murder.

Feel better? Of course you do. For thousands of years boyfriends have been killing their girlfriends' cats, clubbing or stoning them in Neanderthal days, or digging tiny pits with stakes inside, using more devious methods as civilization arose.

History is filled with numerous instances of great kings killing their girlfriends' cats. Alexander the Great's march into Asia Minor, mistakenly thought of by authors as an attempt to create an empire, was merely a disguised means of stomping a cat to death. The legendary Atlantis sank after Greek scientist Kitonius tried to start a small earthquake to eliminate "Hermes," but the reaction got out of hand.

This book will aid you in your mission by presenting the tried and true murder techniques of the masters, including Machiavelli, the Nazi Dr. Mengele, and that all-time great, the Marquis de Sade. Many of the devices described in the following pages are cheaply available at any kill-your-cat shop, which are found in most neighborhoods, if you know where to look. Is there a store or restaurant nearby that never seems to have any customers, yet stays open year after year? Odds are there's a kill-your-cat shop in back. Go in, sit down. When the waiter approaches, drop one or two complaints about the beast. Voilà! A wall will slide open near the kitchen. Be ready to see ways to make your wildest dreams of freedom real.

You love the girl, don't you? You want to stay with her. Remember, behind every successful relationship is a dead cat.

How to Kill Your Girlfriend's Cat

QUICKSAND KITTY LITTER

Here's a quick and odorless way to make your problem disappear. Kitty becomes endangered species in seconds flat. Looks like regular kitty litter, even comes in the same kind of bag. Lighter objects float on top but anything weighing more than a pound sinks down to the oxygenless depths. You go out to the supermarket for one hour. When you come back . . . "Oh, Louis!"

ELECTRIC SCRATCH POST

This handy final solution works on simple transistor radio batteries. It can be shut off with a hidden switch when your girlfriend is in the house, and turned on in seconds when she leaves. When operating, it will shoot nine thousand volts of electricity into anything that touches it. Enough to dispatch the worthless creature, not enough to create a telltale burning smell. Manufacturer's guarantee: The vet will say "heart attack" or money back.

CAT KLUX KLAN

You're relaxing at home one night with your girlfriend, watching TV. Suddenly the door crashes open. Five men in sheets ride in, whooping and carrying torches. They erect a burning cross in the living room. They string up Louis and dance around insanely, singing and drinking. They are gone as quickly as they come, but their parting words linger: "Better not get another cat."

Machiavelli's Trick

Machiavelli never did anything directly. When his girlfriend left the palace for her violin lesson, Machiavelli went to the finest theatrical prop maker in Venice. He ordered two tiny claws constructed, and a set of tiny teeth. While his lover was absent, Machiavelli sneaked into her drawers and closets, using the false claws and teeth to rip up her clothing. Two weeks later, Sonia of Venice ordered "Prince" put to sleep. Today plastic replicas of Machiavelli's devices are available at most kill-your-cat shops. Less likelihood of your girlfriend getting a replacement.

Invite Friends Over

During your visit to the local wrestlers' club, you've made new friends: Ape Morgan, Leif the Carnivore, and Psychopath Jack. Ask them over to "play with the cat." When they stomp out, survey the mangled torso on the floor, put your hands on your hips, and say, "I'm not asking *those* guys over anymore."

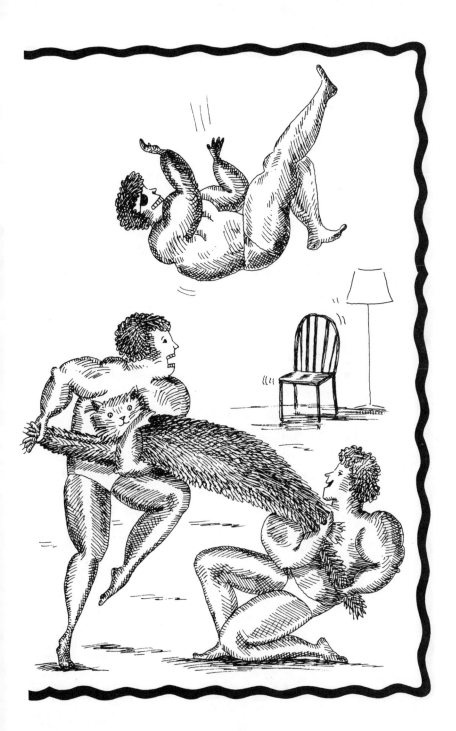

CAT
HIT
MEN
FROM
MINNEAPOLIS

Never mind their names, they get the job done, isn't that enough? And they make it look like an accident. "Gee, honey," you say when you both get back from a day in the country. "The doors are locked. Nothing was stolen. How the heck did the whole wall unit fall on Louis?" To contact the hit men, call the 800 number in the back of this book and say this code sentence. "Hi, do you give distemper shots?"

BOA CONSTRICTOR ESCAPES ZOO! CITY PARALYZED!

A more expensive technique. It requires lots of cash (don't use checks) to print up phony newspapers. Purchase the snake in an exotic pet store. Starve it in the basement for a week. Let it out by the cat's favorite hidey-hole. When the mewing stops, the "rent-a-cop" arrives and promises to "take the snake back to the zoo."

THE "CASK OF AMONTILLADO" SOLUTION

Your girlfriend is remodeling her apartment? And the work's being done while she's at the office all day? Slip the cat a mickey in his Kitty Treats. That night your girlfriend comes home to a candlelight dinner, delicious wine, and flowers. She admires the new wall in the bathroom but thinks she hears scratching on the other side. "Mice," you say. "Tomorrow I'll call the exterminator."

Cat, Trapped in Helium Balloons, Floats Away from New York Apartment

(REPRINTED FROM THE *NATIONAL SCREAMER*)

Louis, a New York cat, was tragically separated from his owner in a most bizarre accident! The sobbing boyfriend told the *Screamer* what happened. "I wanted to surprise her! It was her birthday, I was having a big dinner delivered, and I tied the balloons together and put them on the balcony! Poor Louis must have gotten tangled up in them." Air traffic controllers in Boston believe a recent U.F.O. sighting may have been the unfortunate Louis.

PUT THIS NOTICE UP ALL OVER YOUR NEIGHBORHOOD

"$100 REWARD! Last seen, a gray-and-white cat with a white spot near its nose, eating my Star of India sapphire ring. You'll know it's my ring because of the little diamonds surrounding the sapphire, and the inscription, 'From the Aga Khan. Only the best!' " Put the cat out and wait.

SUBSTITUTE
TRAVELING
CASE

This was the favorite method of Torquemada, the Spanish Inquisitor, for ridding himself of girlfriends' cats. Switch cases just as your girlfriend is leaving with Louis for the airport. Hours later, when it is out of human view in the belly of the plane, *the walls of the case begin to move.* All you have to do is set the timer. The case assumes normal proportions when the deed is done. Looking inside after her trip, your girlfriend asks airline officials, "What's this pancake? Where's Louis?"

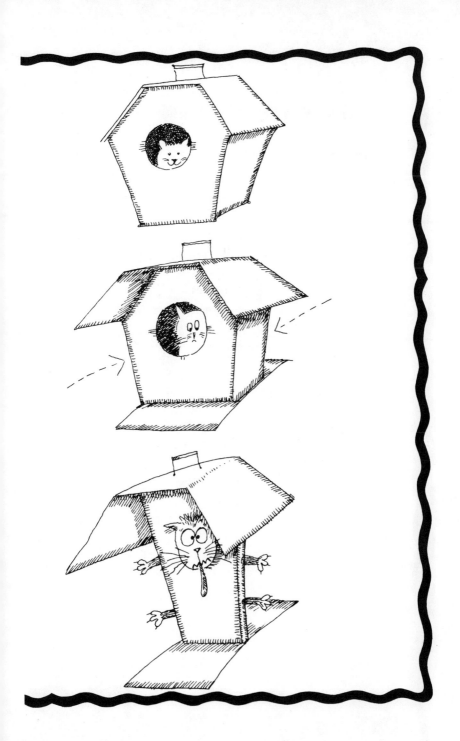

ALLERGY
SHOT

O'H NO! THE CAT GOT RUN OVER BY A TRUCK!

The dreaded Nazi Dr. Mengele invented this device. It guarantees the permanence of a traffic fatality but eliminates the waiting for an accident to happen. Not for the squeamish! Behold! A simple tire-shaped wooden bludgeon, glued to half a genuine tire. Press the device against kitty's belly and roll back and forth, as if making a piecrust. The unmistakable tire marks on the corpse will leave no doubt as to the nature of the accident.

MOUSE ON A STRING

A favorite method used by high-rise cat sufferers. The fishing rod can be purchased at your favorite sporting goods shop. Wear a disguise so that the ASPCA will not track you down later. Any kill-your-cat shop has a huge stock of stuffed mice and birds. Suspend the lure out the window, thirty stories up. The cat is watching. Back and forth. Back and forth. When Louis hits the pavement, dismantle the rod and throw it down the trash chute.

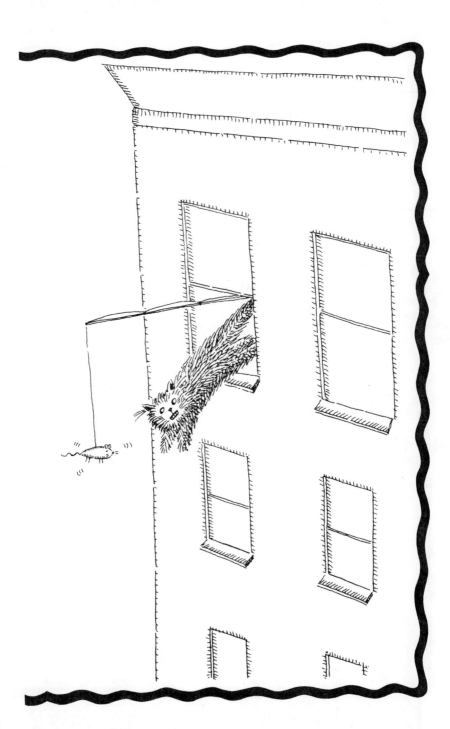

De Sade's Treat

Get the cat's tongue with this genuine replica from the French Revolution. You'll feel like Madame Defarge when you hear the cheery snap, and know the deed is done. The handy pocket combination guillotine, tape recorder produces the fluttering sound of a bird in trouble. Place the device inside a mousehole. Kitty sticks his head inside to take a peek.

VIETCONG THROW TOY

Living in tunnels under the earth during the recent war, and competing with their girlfriends' cats for rats to eat for dinner, the Vietcong would spend hours whittling wooden hand grenades into mouse likenesses. Just pull the pin and toss the toy. Kitty pounces, stares in puzzlement when the "mouse" does not move, and goes to join its honorable ancestors.

CATTILA
THE
HUN

From the catless steppes of northwest Asia.

THINGS TO DO WITH THE CAT AT THE BEACH

CONTINUED

TOP: BODY SURFING

BOTTOM: BURY LOUIS IN THE SAND

THINGS TO
DO
WITH THE
CAT
AT THE
BEACH

TOP: FEED THE FISH

BOTTOM: INTRODUCE LOUIS TO OTHER
SUNBATHERS

Sir
Isaac
Newton
Confirms the
Existence of
Gravity

Breed a
Big
Mouse

Introduce a Natural Enemy into the Environment

THE
WISE
KING
SOLOMON'S
METHOD

Once, in the days of the Bible, two women came to King Solomon. They each claimed to own a cat. "The cat is mine," cried the first woman. The second woman fell on her knees. "No, wise king! It is mine!" Solomon thought a long time. Then he pronounced judgment. "Cut the cat in two, and give half to each woman!" All present claimed this proved the great king's wisdom.

"PIRANHA? I TOLD THAT GUY TO SEND A PIÑATA!"

Make big money filming Louis's demise for a *National Geographic* special! A French ocean-ographer, narrating the grim sequences, would say something like, "Ze cat, one of nature's more curious creatures, mistakes ze fish's hunger for fear. Slowly ze cat lowers one paw into ze water . . ."

When your girlfriend comes home, proudly show her the remains on the bottom of the tank and say, "Look honey! I bought a new toy for the fish. It's next to the little diver! Sea Monster Skeleton!"

CAT-APULT

How the ancient Romans killed girlfriends' cats.

Okay, Who Put the Kitty Treats in the Cuisinart?

The "trail of food" method used by hunters of really big cats in Africa and Asia can be modified for home use. Lay the trail of tasty treats to several possible home appliances. Furnace. Oven. Electrical outlet.

Donate the Cat for Humanitarian Causes

CONTINUED

TOP: NASA Space Program

BOTTOM: Cancer Research

DONATE THE CAT FOR HUMANITARIAN CAUSES

TOP: MINE SAFETY

BOTTOM: PETS FOR STARVING CHILDREN

SICILIAN CAT GRAVEYARD

You'll have hours of gratification mixing cement for this ancient, honorable method. Regular dump-the-cat barges leave hourly from piers in any waterfront town. Remember, use four cement overshoes, not two. Bring your own sack. Louis will be out of your life before you can say "rigor mortis." Afterward, when you've "made your bones," you can tell friends proudly, "Louis sleeps wit da fishes."

How
Benjamin Franklin
Killed
His
Girlfriend's
Cat

Hey Kids! Learn Magic in Your Basement!

CONTINUED

Pick up this special magic kit at any kill-your-cat store. Contains special extra-sharp saw, nitroglycerine, rubber ostrich egg, and twenty sparkling knives. Great Christmas present for nephews or nieces. If your girlfriend has a child, just the perfect thing.

TOP: Saw Cat in Half

BOTTOM: Levitation

Hey Kids! Learn Magic in Your Basement!

TOP: Knife Throw

BOTTOM: Pull an Egg Out of an Ear

EICHMANN
THE
CAT
GROOMER

Catnip
O.D.

INVITE
ANOTHER
COUPLE
OVER WITH
THEIR
CAT TO
PLAY WITH
LOUIS

START A NEW CLOTHING STYLE

Cat jackets are in.

DOUBLE INDEMNITY

In one original version of this classic, Fred MacMurray burned down Barbara Stanwyck's house to collect double indemnity insurance on her cat. Cat lovers forced Hollywood to change the plot, so that a human became the victim. But you can still reenact the original plot.

New Jersey Teen Makes Nuclear Bomb in Basement

(REPRINTED FROM NEW YORK *TIMES*)

East Orange, New Jersey, narrowly escaped destruction Tuesday night when fifteen-year-old Tommy Sty accidentally set off a homemade nuclear device in his house. The mushroom cloud was visible to New Yorkers in the World Trade Center, and Jersey authorities at first believed an earthquake had hit this sleepy suburb. Damage was limited to the obliterated two-story Colonial. The only victim appears to have been Tom's girlfriend's cat, which was staying over for the week.

Take a Taxi to the Dentist? I Thought You Said Taxidermist!

It's true your girlfriend may be irritated by the mix-up at first, but as time passes and Louis remains furry and unchanged, cute as always, reliably there when you want him, and cheaper to maintain by way of food and vet costs, she'll see that it all comes out for the best.

Louis

CATSORCISM

First used in Salem, Massachusetts, during the early settlement of the United States. If you opt for this method, fall on the floor, frothing and rolling your eyes. Chant things like "I saw Louis with the Goody Parker. I saw Louis with the devil!" Soon Father Emmanuel, catsorcist, will be at the door with a tub of holy water. Here's the surefire test. Throw Louis in. If he floats, he's a witch and you must kill him. If he drowns, he wasn't, but who cares?

FAMOUS
MURALS
FROM THE
KILL- YOUR-CAT
ARCHIVES,
WASHINGTON, D.C.

CONTINUED

TOP: ANCIENT EGYPT

BOTTOM: CAVEMEN OF SOUTHERN FRANCE

FAMOUS
MURALS
FROM THE
KILL- YOUR-CAT
ARCHIVES,
WASHINGTON, D.C.

TOP: MACCHU PICCHU

BOTTOM: INDIA

Gaucho
Cat
Roundup
in
Argentina

Genuine bolos can be purchased at any kill-your-cat shop. Cowboy clothes available all over.

Return the Cat to Its Homeland

How could your girlfriend ever hold a grudge against you for such a humanitarian gesture, returning the cat to its natural environment and sacrificing the hours of pleasure you might have had with it so that it can be happy and run free.

Rent-
a-Sadist

Call 1-800-K-I-L-L-C-A-T. A brochure will be mailed discreetly to your office, not your home, in an unmarked brown paper bag. Look over the photos and read the bios. These sadists have been carefully selected from the prisons and dungeons of the world, bonded, licensed, and trained. Hire them as a "cook" or "handyman" for a day. Around these guys, nine lives just isn't enough.

BEFORE AND AFTER

There's much more to successful murder than the actual homicide. "Preparation," said Henry VIII, who killed his wives' forty-five cats, "is the crucial part."

You must change your behavior toward the intended victim for at least two weeks before the act is carried out. Start bringing home toys and treats for the cat. "You know, honey," tell your girlfriend in an awed tone, "I never noticed how blue his eyes were before." And, "Ohhh, look how he lies there, so peaceful and beautiful." Or, "He sure is smarter than a dog, dear. Why, a dog would do anything you ask."

Feed Louis delicious liver snacks, one at a time, by hand. Worry about his health. Say, "Gee, honey," to your girlfriend, "don't his furballs hurt? I better get him to a vet, pronto!" Give the cat pet names like "Friend," "Pal," "Handsome," "Buddy." Tell your girlfriend, "Let *me* feed him today. We'll be better friends that way."

More good quotes. "Look how he watches that fly. He's so alert and useful!" Or, "Darling, I have a confession to make. Ever since I was a baby I've been terrified of sparrows. I feel so much safer with Louis around."

Insist on buying expensive cat food instead of the generic brand. Bring home rubber mice and catnip. Constantly go through the house if you haven't seen him for twenty minutes, fretting, "He might have gotten into a spot." Act jealous if the cat sleeps on your girlfriend's side of the bed. Rush home from nights out because "Louis shouldn't be alone."

All this will make your grief so much more powerful after kitty's demise. At that time rend your clothing. Tear your hair. Collapse, weeping (tears available at any kill-your-cat shop). And cry out, when your girlfriend wants another cat, "No! No! It hurts too much! I can never go through this again!"

Rest assured that these tried and true methods have rid boyfriends of the feline curse throughout the ages. Once the cat is gone, nothing will stand in the way of you and years of happiness.